# LEAVING TRACES

ALSO BY VELMA POLLARD

Poetry

*Crown Point*
*Shame Trees Don't Grow Here*
*The Best Philosophers I Know Can't Read or Write*

Fiction

*Karl and Other Stories*
*Homestretch*

Other Prose

*Considering Woman*

Non-fiction

*Dread Talk: The Language of Rastafari*
*From Creole to Standard*

VELMA POLLARD

# LEAVING TRACES

PEEPAL TREE

First published in Great Britain in 2008
Peepal Tree Press Ltd
17 King's Avenue
Leeds LS6 1QS
UK





ISBN 9781845230210

Peepal Tree gratefully acknowledges Arts Council support

## CONTENTS

WHILE THE SAP FLOWS

# LEAVING TRACES

For Olive Senior and Sybil Francis
and all the women who name things

## PORTOBELLO

I stood
where Drake fell
Francis
forever on my mind

I dont remember
how they say he fell
or who (if anyone) felled him
I only know
forever I have felt
this senior pirate
honoured till my time
remembered still
in names of great hotels
and water passages
deserved to fall

somebody must have said
cutting her eye
"dis wan fi ded bad"
here he died
how bad I cannot tell

green hills look towering down
on that fair strand
that looks in turn out to a tranquil sea
from ancient look-outs standing
still (remembering all the El moro
signatures of Spain)

now little children
clamber  up the ramp
looking at cannons
touching their rusted mouths

free from all fear
(the smell of powder
fired from these guns
envelops all my air)

no tablet holds his name
only ancestral murmurs
mouthing words
remind me
here he died
aquí  se murió
el falleció
these words in syllables
his spirit does not recognize

yet it is fitting that he should die here
(unless he could die everywhere)
here where a tract of land
links the Atlantic and Pacific
here where best re-
presents all island histories
new nomads wandering...

how could Drake know
that galleons would bring here
slaves yearning to fulfill
dreams that were dreamt
before their fathers' futures
dreams to construct
the awesome interlocking
locks lakes
Canal
that would connect
Carib and South sea
(against divine design?)

this jut of land
making the two worlds one

so here I stand
smelling the blood of Drake
smelling gun power
seeing mingled sailors soldiers
spirits pushing metal...
feeling this deep and
satisfying end
conclusion to some things

Drake did die here
and while I smile
small children stare and wonder
whispering underneath their hands
"la loca"

## MUSINGS ACROSS FROM THE PORT AUTHORITY

*(Charlotte Amalie)*

I every time
I land
from far by plane
or near by ferry
feel this urge to
print on paper, photograph
roofs fitted step by step
one on the other
like a Kapo city
or that forever Haitian village
painted on cheap calico
on every corner
of a hungry Port au Prince
black houses
stark on ochre calico
or painted bright in yellow red and blue
selling for cents
or just enough to buy a meal

awesome that sense of scale
awesome here roof on roof
topography is all
or is it?

Don't ask the Haitian mother selling
roofs like these on calico
selling against her children's *tireless hunger*

don't ask her brother canvas-bag in hand
boarding the boat that may or may not reach
Miami or Exuma
taking his chance
to leave

the poorest country in the hemisphere (?)
while you (an island too) are spoken for
by Uncle rich and powerful
up north there

topography is nothing then
but chimera
search history page on page
ask pointless questions
try to understand the hows and whys

grandchildren of a proud Toussaint
are mendicant on dirty streets while you
offspring of orphans auctioned cheaply by the Danes
revel in opulence and opportunity

are you no longer orphans though
and they no longer slaves?
is look-alike more after all
than mere topography?

all in compassion ends
so differently…
from what whose heart arranged?

## JUAN BAUTISTA 1998

Here in Loiza
hordes no longer
gather
waiting to baptize
to stave off evil with sea water

(in Spain, I hear, they walk over
fire)

few families
under the shadow of palm trees
and new wind
fight paralyzing heat

families with barbecues
babies and

teen-agers

romp where waves break
warmly near the shore

come midnight
these few adults
will close their eyes
dip three times backwards
wish whatever wish they wish
on silent lips

remembering years
when large crowds
Bomba music
mixed with wishes here

no Bomba now
sound-
boxes belt out
young ones
try to learn

Reggae (the sound of kings?)

displacing
Bomba drum men
come from here

come sad now
say tradition
needs its honouring
must be handed down

how else to keep?

I humble
come from reggae land
to honour Bomba
cant believe
this cultural conquest
bow my shamefaced head

old folks
regale me
tales of Bomba
song and dance
and how
sounds used to be
before the bridge
bringing the city near

bringing the night-
mare he had feared
the old man said

I want to smash the globe
(squeezing his hand)
I said

## THINKING RE-THINKING BATHS, VIRGIN GORDA

I : (1987)

Peter as rock
(on which I build my church)
was good enough for Christ
in Palestine

here rocks build
Cathedrals
a thousand times the breadth of man
ten times his height

the Father playing blocks
with rocks

sometimes they are ample beds
whose canopies are trees

and sometimes rooms
where lovers hide from envious eyes

sometimes they fall into the bay
make sandy coves

these baths
that give this rest its name

where little children fearless
dive from rock to sea floor
laughing

II (1988)

Batholith
its rocks
now lit with sun shafts
beaming over myriad
baylets

bathers
each in his own cove
bask in its salt
sand and crystal sea

who knows how sprang
these rocks from out the deep
or when ?

who knows how soon
these rocks return
to sea floor why?

centuries of calm
will hear their low complaints
gurgling like sea-shelled water
how little children
scrambling up
chipped bone away
leaving serrated edges

how drunken boaters
entering from the sea
flung beer cans wine casques
stuck there now
these shards of copper colour
faking nature
art by chance

while creatures ever sea-borne
hold their sides and laugh
and unbelieving whisper
underneath serrated hands
lies  lies...

III (1998)

Again these awesome rocks
this Batholith
these Baths
that terrify and soothe

again this helpless
facing nature towering here
how small a thing is (wo)man

mark the cool
early morning silence
all human out of sight

lying low perhaps
in boats riding at anchor
or circling the slow bay

lying low
to wonder at the sea carved
face of giant rock on rock

Later the sun comes
bringing Columbuses
with back-packs and blubber
gazing at rocks they dare not climb
(footholds too few and far between
rockface too smooth)

close your eyes
listen and hear
waves breaking gently near the shore
inhaling loud
exhaling soft

until the boom box
cracks the almost silence

Music however sweet
disturbs the meditative mood
beach and the Baths get littered now
selling T-shirts
with music sun and ice

# MONTSERRAT

*(May 1998)*

*I: Old Town*

curtains still move
where wind blows
cooling windows

yards swept
doors barely shut...

parents will come
home here

anytime  now
children banging lunch pans
will prance  up these
stone steps
hurry to rooms
throw school bags down
rush out...

No

for the ash is piled
in heaps
where flowers and weeds
fight for supremacy

and neither child
nor parent
will come home

a bar divides
safe from unsafe

the hill slide is smooth
unrumpled
where liquid turned ash
poured down

and unlittered
except for bare bones
here and there

the town is silent
like sleep

while Vesuvius of the Antilles
still smokes
ever so slightly

II

Tourist board posters
in cruel irony
shout still
"The way the Caribbean used to be"

the golf course
grass light even green
on each side trees
dark and lush green

and poincianna
painted bright orange and red

(the hawk eyed putter
club at ready
barely checks his swing)

water
falls white with blue
on towering rocks
where clinging withe and low moss
keep their precarious hold...

Today I saw
that golf course
even grey
sprinkled with pebbles
near the shore
no longer beach
where little boats sit
weak from unemployment

and I will never see the water
falling white with blue

clean covered over now
gone underground
a cistern for the mountain house perhaps
the waterfall is gone
elsewhere water is born

I saw a new beach
miracle
metallic slate grey sand
confessing origins
within the bubbling hill

a beach kissed constantly
by light and faithful foam
there where aeroplanes arriving
and departing droned yesterday

volcanic liquid cooled to powder
rolled down the very hill whose side is turned to me
into the sea
where feisty waves
rushed in to claim it
took it where they wished...

waves calm now
brush this beach
in quiet song
beside a silent runway

The archipelago
shaped and reshaping underneath our eyes

a thousand Virgins come to mind
formed when volcanoes burst from under water
forcing  beach to hill
now eons later mountain ash makes  beach

who will be next we ask
which rainbow island goes
which comes

(breach Jenny harassing boats
is kicking to be born near Carriacou)

beauty and change and terror
all are one

## GREAT FOREST, DEBRECEN

Remembered shadows
walk beside me
here in Debrecen

alone but not alone
in the (really not so great)
Great Forest
watching king trees
sensing on either side
men towering tall
protecting fears
and filling silences

talking of words
talking of rocks
talking of trees

and so I know
and tell the world
that memory is the senior gift

II

Sun leaves
on terraced paths
make fractals

on stone seats in the shade
young men make patterns
tracing young girls' faces

young men
play hand and footsies
fondling fingers
touching toes
and young girls
dont resist

this touch of nature
here in Debrecen
making the whole world kin

## AT THE HORTOBAGY NEAR DEBRECEN

*(for Cecile Carrington)*

Sheep
with light brown curly hair
laze here
like sheep
at ease

in pens
with patient pigs
whose mane
lies straight and black...

Unloading from the
horse-drawn buses
us...
from many countries
gawk
at sheep
with brown and curly hair

creole I say
mixed breed
hybrid
high breed
of language
people
sheep now

creole sheep
I say
these pigs are parents
too

scornful
they answer
doesn't she know
species dont mix

creole
I stubbornly repeat
sheep

Science
without imagination
quite ignores
the likes of Minos
Leda with the swan
or Hindu
Ganesh with his elephant head

still science cant defeat
(I think/ wink)
white sheep black pigs
oink oink

in heat

## FOR GIOVANNA

*(before Trento)*

It snowed
the day they put my father in

(why after such a sunshine for his requiem?)

the sun shone bright
to send my mother out

snow fell unseasonably
when they put her in

arrayed in white
they went

snow  symbol
welcome there

leaving the  brilliant
Mantuan yellow here

## TRENTO

*(Fall 2000)*

I

no radio yet
so music here
is rain
and rain itself
is foreground
background
base notes and treble
trembling
fortissimo
to cobbled streets
enticing
easy sleep

until
the shattering TV truth
of rivers
giving up their banks
and thousands newly homeless

weather- mongers
sigh and wonder
when and where
the Po will empty out itself

the rain
entices me no longer
now I watch and sleep
and struggle to believe
the last great
finalizing flood
was Noah's

II: *Rain*

This rain...
she said

I spent
I said

September once
in England

Strange
I watched
the river
flood
the flood
like huracán
Trento
October

October
I sighed
all over

you brought
the rain
she said
we  never...

November can
and has
I said
but who can prove
the mind's
prediction

till the eye
storms in

III: *Train to Venice*
(for Evan Wilson)

Sticks
like crossed swords
protect the grapes
for mile on mile
beside the Adige

this river
gentle now
the last week's
threatening turbulence
turned history

beyond
rock mountains
making castles, temples, shipyards
cities of the mind
with here and there a real one
(castle)
firmly stowed

It is October now
no snow
or very little on the peaks
sunlight and bright pink foliage
peep from over rock
from time to time

From Rivereto
Venice bound
this dream
some thirty years begun

Catullus' gem
(O Sirmio

paene insula)
yesterday's surprise

Sirmio
where vowels stretch
and curl up at the end
closer to Rome that sound
than Celtic Trent
with its teutonic blend

Today's is Venice
ancient waterways
and hand shined gondolas
now worth their weight in gold
Piazza San Marco
higglers here
like cities everywhere
the same fake brands
the same importunate hands

the Rialto
remembering Shylock
and his crowd
then the trattoria
almost hidden
in the cool arcade
treat of Venetian fish

and later
in and out the
several other arcades
to Tiepolo's scuola...

at home
Tiepolo's Walcott hound
sits waiting...

IV: *On the corner  in Trento*

Perhaps a book
in hand
to say
this wistful woman
standing
is not
soliciting

no sister
seeking  favours
just a woman
waiting
on the corner
by the bread shop
(paneficio: I make
efficient bread!)

where a car
her friend
will pass
and take her
anytime now
home

(cant take her
from her door
a city door
on favoured
cobbled streets
where rules say
cars cant come)

She's old
you say

and street women
are young
but who
I ask you

who will guess
a woman's age here
where she's black
(you've seen one
haven't you
further south
in a museum)

men  yes
arms full
of trays
with trinkets
selling

no
pretending that they sell
set up with dignity
black  beggars
ageless
after apple-
picking
waiting to go home
to Senegal, Algeria
any Africa

But they are men
so tell me then
how should
a woman look

perhaps a book...

# DOUBLE VISION

## CUT LANGUAGE!

*(for Stephen )*

Wrapping your tongue
round words
Stephen man-
oevering
"spinsters and
bachelors"

how many learn to spell
but never practise
words
my grandson

you will be
wordsman
claiming this English
language
other people's
anguish

claiming our
patwa

switching easy
when reason calls
"I saw the lightning
leaping through the house
I heard the thunder clap
an Nanny bawl out ' Jiizas Krais'"

Children across the wall
offend
and you defend
with "gwe bwai

no bada wi"

didn't I tell them
everytime
bilingual is the lick?

## PICASSO'S RAPE SERIES (PONCE '98)

*(After* Breath Eyes and Memory *for Maria Cristina)*

I celebrate
Picasso

Pablo
King-painter
politician
man

but these sketches
if they mark him
make him
macho
monster
chauvinist

*Rape one*

drawn simple figure of a driven man
rushing towards this mound
this myriad breasts and thighs

later two bodies caged
the female fighting
arms and legs

to loose
thighs breasts and legs
arms flailing/fighting

failing
hopeless

charged against man's force
and implement

*Rape two*

the pattern changes
now man's mind
confuses parts
rounding whatever
can be round
all breast and buttocks

*Rape under the window*

that mind of man
confuses parts again
lengthening whatever
can have length
all arms and legs

*Violation IV*

this next
most horrid and
most powerful
buttocks and rounded thigh
becoming
brain its
serial segments
flesh and sinew here

a woman's brain
a mind confused

and terrified
the horrid bull man's head
peeps out
established in her brain…

forever and forever
she will dream
and dreaming will forever
pierce the quiet night
wild with desolation
a million nightmares
drive her
to her sleepless end

*Rape V*

her tortured hair undone
mixes with arms and legs
urgent in threatened flight
all body trying still
in vain
to expel the harsh and forceful
muscled skin

*Rape VII*

bodies conmingled
buttocks arms
arms back and thigh
no part distinct
except the man's head
clearly sketched
and separate now
But look

this time
the man himself
shows horror in his eyes ...

What are they doing Dad ?
the small girl asks
the father
tracing arms and legs with fingers
(do not touch)

What can a father say?
they are fighting
he half lies

## IT IS THE DYING TIME

*(for Madge Hall)*

It is the dying time
the tall boy writes
counting the dead...

bird on the wing
moves lightly
near the purple sunset deepening

blissful and carefree
bird cannot know
how keen the short boy aims

(another David
with his sling)

This bird
is not Goliath
large and sure

wounded near night
she falls  her gentle head
against a stone

## SCHISTOSOMA

*(for Emily Krasinski)*

Schistosoma
swims through toe spaces
from rivers moving slow
down the archipelago
up through yards of gut

and men with ten toes
innocent of leather
are sitting water ducks

Abijah soon sits nodding
like Taata waiting on his sentence home
or hands still resting lightly on the hoe
dreams off

and even I
parrotting Maasa's verbiage
want to know
bwai how you can sleep so?

He died too soon

I weep
now that I know
the nodding nigger
Schistosoma

had

to nod so

## WHILE TV TOWERS BURN

*(Fall 2001)*

I

Is someone out there saying
now they know?

ghosts nodding out there
now they feel

flames frightening
guiltless sisters
brothers blinded
smoke and dust
and shock?

Who's bombing?
where's burning
London? Berlin?
Iraq, Iran or madmen in Grenada?

a morning's nightmare here

The Pentagon, New York's twin
towers of brick and steel

Who's screaming
why the answering tears ?

"It's literally chaos now out there" reporting
reporting reporting
from PS which
school teacher
voices calm
across the inter-
com/e tell

little children
how to
where to
hide

Two planes hit
mokojombie tower
twins a hundred stories
high
screech of
women's voices
ambulances
fire-
trucks casualties...

firemen and cops
go answering children
pointing where to
not to
go

smoke smoke
and flames
remembering
Montserrat puffing
dark grey clouds and
Aetna flaming orange
Summer skies

ring the brigade bell
toll for three hundred dead
firemen charging
brave up stairwells
bright to their last

fire this time!

II

The head of the hydra is cut
The heads of the hydra are springing

Tell them  but will they hear?

You come to me with a sling and a stone?
Goliath deriding died

You tell them
Me they wont hear

high passion pass high tech
for driven and driver are one

tell them but they wont hear
tell them but they dont care

So they bomb the stone mountain
Crack open caves

yesterday survivor was a million dollar dare
today survivor is empty handed, spared

throw the dice now and see
whose luck is out
whose luck is in
terror is terror anywhere
Iran, New York

Port Royal's wreck
so many fathoms deep
(where earth shook up
and not a ripple on the sea)

show them
but will they see?

Hospital people
huddle now
caring the dying:

plane blast
stone splatter
or backlash

as we (?) stab
one young white nigger-
loving bastard visiting (from Australia?)

one harmless ageing uncle
Sikh minding his petrol
station without flames etc. etc.

screaming
America
America
they ask
why innocent
we must defend
a turban
or the right to choose a friend?

III

"Lest we become the evil we deplore..."
this from the Holy Pulpit
the Lord Bishop pleads
to folks and terrorists
the Other from the flaming chair of power finger points
"If you are the friend of my enemy you are my enemy;
our targets have no bases but their harbourers have..."

So mothers' hair will tangle with the dust
falling for sons they never bore
so You can find that face or any face
to take your anger and your hate

Ben Laden
friend turned foe
moonwalks his TV
walk of yesteryear

this face we know
this face we can
recurring scan
long evenings in the family room

the little voice
the powerless voice
insists to deafened ears
"an eye for an eye leaves both men blind"

and so
we going to
bomb them
smoke them
root them out

For collateral damage:

old peoples homes
creches and hospitals
we deeply apologize.

IV

New York, New York
our new connection is to absence
this ash that was our desks our e-mails
and our friends…

shards of sharp glass
of concrete and of bone
mingle with ash
confusing …

striving to reconstruct
we construct stretchers
find no wounded for them
body bags no bodies to fill them

faithful
fearful hands
dreading to dredge
find foot
traumatic hand here
debris and their dust

V

No need for Halloween this year.
this year the earth has brought
(has bought)
its own dry pestilence of ash

this hallows eve
cinders smoke still
in zero plaza once New York

dust burns to ash
in bombed out stone
seeking out Talibans
the turbaned men
of nightmare Whatsitstans

stone ground to ash
powders the envelopes
proliferating fear
proliferating Anthrax
on our air

that air that
flew the planes
that brought the bombs
that crushed the stone
that made the ash
that choked the

little children
babies
stifling
still
in half-bombed
hospitals
near Pakistan

Circle of ash
Kabul to Kentagon
Pabul to Pentagon

witches this year
treat ashes
tricking Anthrax
on new friendships
sour treaties

turning our ash
on our own proper
entrails
complicating  grief

now forward to
Iraq (?)

## WAR CHILD

*(after Iraq)*

For weeks and weeks before the war
while war threats thundered in the air
I worried
focused on that
globe eyed kindergarten boy
laughing and running
carefree with the wind…
that playground in Tikrit

and on his wide-eyed sister
hugging goodbye
and kissing him
then sheltering clutching
mother's flowing skirt

and after mosque on Friday
friends and family
stealing glances at their innocence…
what if the soldiers freed them?
what if tomorrow?

while macho power brokers
Tweedlebush and Tweedleblair
hugging their own
less wide-eyed
thin-lipped children
plotted freedom

And now my little wide-eyed friend
liberated
lost
groaning in pointless pain
wordlessly wonders

why  the boy soldier
sitting near his bed
in this strange hospital
( in Kuwait?)
talks about freedom
in such poor Arabic

why is he smiling?

hallucinations
after nurse's ministration
take my once bright friend
laughing and running
(without arms and legs)
far from the friendly soldier

to that windy playground
in  Tikrit

# MESSIAH

They say the Messiah will come
someday
perhaps today

and if he comes
when he comes
in Gaza

or looking for
Bethlehem
where

they say
the fake precursor
was born

if he too wants
to live
to be thirty three

which of the men in the mosque
who with his bayonet drawn
which of the frightened faces

is He?

WHILE THE SAP FLOWS

## WHILE THE SAP FLOWS

April comes in
with yellow poui
defining Mona

and this one leafless trunk
a young amputee
basket case
lately returned
(from which wind- war?)
shoots
from out naked nodes
its brilliant yellow blooms

the sap still flows

blooms hug the trunk
that shouts out
I too can!

echoing its note
amidst the yellow branches
of those luckier trunks
who shower their myriad petals
blanketing the earth

And what a message
there for us
whose strides
each early morning
take us past this place

Know this
O doubting heart
that while the sap flows
there is nothing
man cannot

## VIEW UP THROUGH HER WINDOW

*(for Olive Senior)*

There is an oak in her garden
with maple behind

green leaves
on purple
figure on blue sky ground

and there is quiet here
except when bird sounds
struggle with aeroplanes
droning to fade away
finally

or bird flutes fuse
with bass of aeroplanes
and the percussive shrrr shrrr
of wind drumming leaves
light with soft fingertips

In the Fall
she will plant anemones
gardening
no longer in the tropics

gardening and paying for advice
here where no grand-
fathers unasked
instruct us
how and what to plant

Gardening
is costly here

and cold

## SOURSOP/ TREE  I REMEMBER

A boy swings deftly from the branch
toes graze my head
then barely touch the ground
"so sorry Ma'am"
then roll roll stop

eyes closed
hands still now
(boy playing dead?)
slowly his chest…
heave out
heave in

"failed tumbletud" I laugh and sing
straddling the tree crotch V
where limb meets limb

These leaves I look at now
green velvet polished by the sun
another several years
will lie
crumpled and brown
beneath some other body
hiding in the shade

birds flit
and salivate
the future peck
the future fruit

tonight
green leaves
home-brewed

with honey
hush tired thoughts
sooth tired limbs
to sleep

## CLOUDS

*(for Stephanie)*

Like ducks on blue ponds
like swans at sea
like cotton floating
falling anywhere

like candy floss
like myriad brides
in simple white

like choir boys
like cherubim

clouds
like everything

## BIRDSONG

Moving from under-
mountain house
into the concrete city
jostling  townhouses
business houses
banks and prostitutes
I heard me say
I surely will miss birds

but early that first day
and every morning after
brown doves
ground doves
serenade each other
either side of my verandah

Eavesdropping  I
hover hiding
round the corner
hearkening bird sounds
like bird song sounding
every morning sweetly
near my under-
mountain house

now here
then there
they neither know nor care
how my heart thrills
as their songs thrill each other's heart
and gently sweetly also wake the town

between bird kisses
before the sun comes out

before the urgent clatter
garbage trucks, route- taxis
buses signaling that other
harsher life
the town

I ( and some clear -eared others)
hear them
love them
thank them

everyday

they make my day
in town

## FALL LEAVES

*(by bus to Binghamton)*

Barely one yellow
Fall leaf left

barren brown stalks
call Winter in

leaves stripped to mesh
to skeleton
and tree feet standing
unshod in dry
leaves  dying
flat on their faces

wind curls them on their sides
train their dry eyes
briefly on branches
curved from there
like sea fans

Yesterday those branches
clutched vainly at their stems
whispering with tears "dont leave, dont go"

nature so fragile here
and urgent
leaves must fall
and branches weep
and seem to break

and then to Spring again
young other leaves

branches must clutch

those new loves
fondly
say again next Fall
with tears “dont leave”

## PHASE II

This next time round
we face the union with more sureness
less fragile hope
less pressuring either "I"
no forced entwinement into one
but closeness
and our separate selves

this next time round
a calm maturity
forgets the nervous eagerness of youth

a less demanding king
I ask no sacrifice
a now securer queen
you ask no reassurance in required lies

a gentle turbulence envelops us
a twilight lovelier than the midday sun

"ripeness is all"

## FAREWELL

I

Always when the night is calm
when only the swish of waves
patting the sand
sounds through the silence

you comfort my spaces

peace without words
without touch
strength without presence

through you
spirit man
Massa God proves

He doesn't always come
Sometimes He does send

II

Sweetheart
I heard me say
and no time to retract

twin engines puttering
rushed pilots cockpitting

Friend
I hope you understand
Agape
borrowing by chance
Eros' vocabulary

## UNREPENTANT HETERO

here amid these sisters
some vehemently
most gently
affirming
confirming
pleasures of passion
"that leaves no traces"

homoerotic
I
listen and
wish I could
tell them
that you too
leave no traces

hands
gentle approving
touch
tender improving
this body
leaving no traces

marks dont show
on marrow
where deep stirrings grow

## SCORE EVEN

that other time
amid the music
and the crowd
I felt her fling her flesh
a heavy slab
from breast to belly-button
meant for him

she so desperate…

and now I recollect
I did not smile
and open up the circle
let her in
but simply swung back in
from out
the music guiding

Down the years
I heard her hurt eyes
watch me
jam with him

tonight the hurt is mine
that same flesh now
throws centre
her eyes laugh

me now despairing

orphaned from his care
find shelter in my art

## HOMELESS

Your home?
he asked

I led him to the place
half boxes
blocks
and other people's
cast off curtains
haphazard

Rolling up his sleeves
he set the blocks in order
raised the bed
( a cast off sofa really)
hoisted the string
that held the curtain
pulled it to the end

card-boarded holes
that let eyes in
sealed up each space that let in
rain and sky
straightened the window
heaped odd remains
"building materials"
in one pile

and finally
finding a coconut broom
he swept the littered
hardened earth...
I smoothed the sofa
stuck two yellow cushions on

he stretched his full height
touched the roof
then bending from the waist
smiling he said
"your flat madam"
and led me to the bed

## CONFESSIONS OF A SON

My father lost me
somewhere between
the smell of leather
shoes and the enchantment of untying laces

Waiting to cross swords
with the tyrant
who would cow her
I man watched
hovering over
Mother

(I four feet high)
standing on tiptoe

Half century later
still I do not know
if culture curbed concern
or if he loved less
than he needed love

I store for her
affection without question
for him respect
with unlove
waiting for compassion

## SINGLE MOTHER

She's toiling up
five flights of stairs
bags  in her hands
lead in her heart

The little faces peering at the top
(careful to keep the chain on)
shout with glee
Mumeeeeeeeee

But they are four
last Summer they were three

What did he tell you
Mother
how concoct
a tale so sweet
that you would lie
and calmly let him in?

What words have you prepared
what actions then
or will you
every winter
let him  in
till there are ten?

## CASSANDRA

She sits there
old
a new peace
fitted on her face

that frown
the agony of non-fulfilment
gone

the oh so pretty girl
whose head pull up
the daughter
tells her own life
loudly

man/no man
child
without father
world without end

tells of prized sister
blood turned against her
bright body shrinking
(while foreign doctors watch
and shake their heads
in wild despair)

she's going home, they say
far far away from home

And so they sit there
fading beauty
with decaying age
near pavements

sinking to the earth
unkempt verandahs
looking out at walls
falling and almost dead

But she smiles now
and sets me free

## CONFESSION

*"Mine eyes have seen what my hands did"*
*Lowell*

I heard
the crowd
shout murderer

A gentle child-
like face
he stared at me

I stared at him
come nearer Sar
he said

I know yu face
my father
first gun
from your hand

I see yu give him
hear yu tell him gun-
man business
haffi do

My business too
until this crowd
decide...

dem woulda chop mi up
like meat
policeman save me...

So Sar
I a ask yu now
yu didn tink...?

My lowered eyes
now see
what my hands did

# MY CATHOLIC COUSIN

My Catholic cousin makes rosaries
rosaries for Catholics in heathen
Paraguay
Uruguay
Chile and Equador

my Catholic cousin is dying
she is calling for her daughter

who is making crosses
crosses to keep out devils

devils she says are Catholics
Pope-worshipping people

people in her church bear
witness for Jehovah

my Catholic cousin is dying calling for
her daughter
who is cursing so she cannot answer
her mother

she is cursing Catholics everywhere
Paraguay, Uruguay the USA etc. etc.
but especially in Italy
because the Pope
chief devil
lives there

she cannot speak to the devil
so the daughter cannot answer her mother

Who can release that mother
who will release
my Catholic cousin
to die without anguish
close her eyes
fade away
into peace
without anguish?

Holy Mary
Mother of God
pray for us
pray for us all
sinners
now and at the hour of our death

## OUT OF JOINT

out of joint
young men
spit spite
on fathers
and on fathers fathers

out of joint
shooting wild word
wild bullet
wild intent
silence God men
God women
whose good words
good deeds
lighten  our loads

heaven
through muted horns
sounds us her warning
rain where before no rain
torrents and storms
raging while
good crops freeze and burn

heedless we rush
ears stuck un-
hearing
plugged   no doubt

this time
is out of joint

## MID-LIFE

accept the midlife challenge
celebrate...

but days fly fast now
after Easter
Christmas comes
before you say Jack Robinson
or Kwame King

how brief mid-
life how soon
is evening
golden age
(or rage?)

and feebleness sets in
the bones complain
too much ...
the mind complains
too many queries

see now
that web site
search is slow
sharpness is only memory

the future hobbles in
on crook stick
does not fly
on witch's broom

the moving finger pointing
angles closer
to the wrinkled skin

look out
All Souls/All Saints
we coming

all hearts
look out
let's celebrate
the now

## WITH THANKS

*(...ya estamos muertos cuando nada nos toca,*
*ni una palabra, ni un anhelo, ni una memoria...”*
*Jorge Luis Borges)*

Somewhere between my soul’s brief waking and its death
we loved
blending the moon’s eye with our wonder
somewhere between my borrowed youth and its thereafter
we touched
and marvelled
fortunados

So when my delta years
their gentle sands run
warm between your fingers
my skin reflecting my soul’s glow
will smooth forgetful of time’s touch
and all the marrow of November bones
will warm
remembering
how we loved

## ABOUT THE AUTHOR

Velma Pollard was born in Jamaica in 1937, educated at Excelsior High School in Kingston and at the University College of the West Indies. She received an MA in Education from McGill University and an MA in the teaching of English from Columbia University. She taught in high schools and universities in Jamaica, Trinidad, Guyana and the USA. Since 1975 she has taught at the University of the West Indies, Mona. She retired as Senior Lecturer in Language Education and Dean of the Faculty of Education of the University of the West Indies.

She has always written. She won her first prize for a poem at the age of seven, but none of her work went beyond her desk until 1975 when encouraged by her sister Erna Brodber and others, notably Jean D'Costa who sent one of her stories to *Jamaica Journal*, she started sending pieces to journals in the region. She published *Crown Point and Other Poems* and *Shame Trees Don't Grow Here* with Peepal Tree in 1988 and 1992 respectively. *Considering Woman*, a collection of prose pieces was published by The Women's Press in 1989. Her novella *Karl* won the Casa de las Americas in 1992. Her monograph, *Dread Talk - the Language of the Rastafari* was published in 1994 by Canoe Press. She has also edited several anthologies of writing for schools.

She is the mother of three children.

An interview with Velma Pollard appears in Daryl C. Dance *New World Adams: Conversations with Contemporary West Indian Writers*.

## ALSO BY VELMA POLLARD

*Crown Point*
ISBN:9780948833243; pp.: 84; £7.99

*Crown Point* is the first and long overdue collection of poems by one of the Caribbean's foremost woman poets. Velma Pollard's poems range from affectionate and observant family portraits to the righteous anger of an Afro-Caribbean woman's truth telling. *Crown Point* closes with a moving series of poems that meditate on death, mourning and their meaning for the living. They speak both of the deaths of parents and grandparents and of 'deaths falling early' and hear always Anancy's susu susu whispering words, 'tiday fi mi/ tumaro fi yu'. These are poems which have a quiet, consoling truthfulness, no answers, just the unvarnished reminder that this is the way of life and that the dead remain with us: 'No one philosophy can answer all/ each man is an island/ each mind is a muffin tin/ and so we sit with our invisible pencils/ working out strategies to cope with brevity/ to cope with our adieux/ to love – too sweet to forget/ to life – too intense to leave...' These tender elegiac poems of loss and remembrance have an eloquent stillness at their heart. All share a common depth of reflection and concern with poetic craft.

'Reading... Velma Pollard is to encounter an acutely sensitive consciousness grappling, even in apparently lighter moments, with the complexity of experience.' – Evelyn O'Callaghan, *Jamaica Journal*.

*Shame Trees Don't Grow Here*
ISBN: 9780948833489; pp. 72; £7.99

A shame tree is a Jamaican symbol for the development of moral consciousness, and the poems in this collection explore the points at which moral values emerge – and the consequences of their absence. The poems suggest toughly that such consciousness does not grow without unremitting effort and scrupulous sensitivity to feeling, but there is nothing didactic or moralistic about them. They are imaginative recreations of the dramas of coming to consciousness and the inevitable ambiguities of truth. As in all Velma Pollard's work, there is a deeply imbued sense of Caribbean history.

Marvin Williams writes in *The Caribbean Writer*: 'Tone and emotion range wider in Velma Pollard's *Shame Trees Don't Grow Here... but poincianas bloom* – from disgust, anger, and outrage to celebration, awe, and praise; from questioning and condemnation to understanding and reconciliation. The major thrust of the poet's fire comes in the first part of the book where those who lacked or are lacking conscience and moral boundaries are drawn into Pollard's unflinching scrutiny. Wildfire becomes hearth in part two where the beauty and life-enhancing qualities of land, sea, and people are celebrated. Throughout, the poet's skillful use of language remains evident in, for example, her subtle, unobtrusive rhymes that lend musicality to her verse; her puns; double entendres; and other word play.'

All Peepal Tree titles are available from the website
**www.peepaltreepress.com**
with a money back guarantee, secure credit card ordering and fast delivery throughout the world at cost or less.

Peepal Tree Press is celebrated as the home of challenging and inspiring literature from the Caribbean and Black Britain. Visit www.peepaltreepress.com to read sample poems and reviews, discover new authors, established names and access a wealth of information. Subscribe to our mailing list for news of new books and events.

Contact us at:
Peepal Tree Press, 17 King's Avenue, Leeds LS6 1QS, UK
Tel: +44 (0) 113 2451703 E-mail: contact@peepaltreepress.com